Introduction to Cyber Security

simpli|learn

MW00882787

Secure Enterprise Architecture and Component

simpli**learn**

Learning Objectives

By the end of this lesson, you will be able to:

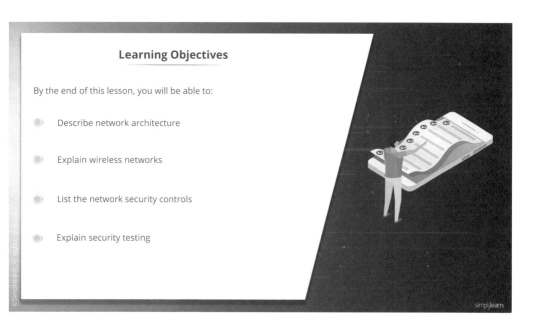

- Describe network architecture

- Explain wireless networks

- List the network security controls

- Explain security testing

simpl¦learn

FULL STACK

Network Architecture

simplilearn

Enterprise Network Architecture

Networks are part of a large, centrally managed, and internetworked architecture solutions.

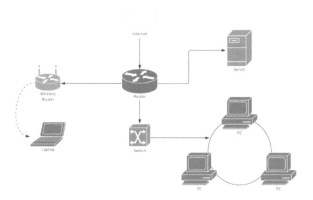

Enterprise Network Architecture

Web-based front-end
application servers

Application and database
servers

Mainframe servers

simpl**i**learn

Enterprise Network Architecture

Organizations implement service-oriented architectures (SOA) with web software components.

Simple Object Access Protocol (SOAP)

Extensible Markup Language (XML)

Basics of Network Architecture

Telecommunications:
Electromagnetic transmission of data

Protocol:
A standard set of rules

Types of Network Architecture

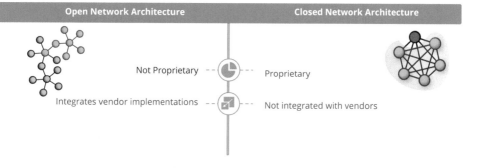

Open Network Architecture	Closed Network Architecture
Not Proprietary	Proprietary
Integrates vendor implementations	Not integrated with vendors

Open System Interconnection (OSI) Model

simpli**learn**

Open System Interconnection (OSI) Model

OSI is a layered architecture.

Simplifies the network design

Helps in easier network management

Helps in debugging network applications

Seven Layers of OSI Model

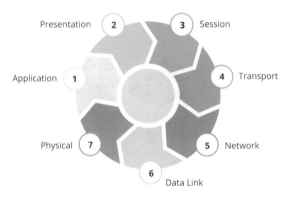

Types of Networks

simpl,learn

Types of Networks

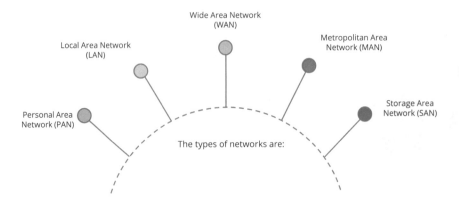

Wide Area Network
(WAN)

Local Area Network
(LAN)

Metropolitan Area
Network (MAN)

Personal Area
Network (PAN)

Storage Area
Network (SAN)

The types of networks are:

Data Communication Systems

simpl¦learn

Data Communication Systems

A process of using computing technology to transfer data from one point to another.

Data Communication Systems:
Transfers digital data between nodes
Uses ASCII, EBCDIC, and Unicode for conversion

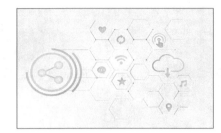

Data Communication Software Components

Information to be communicated

The components of communication software are:

Sender and receiver

Medium or channel

simpli learn

FULL STACK

Computer-Based and Business Information Systems

simpl**|**learn

Computer-Based Information System

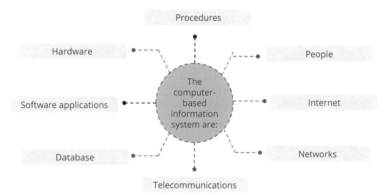

Business Information Systems

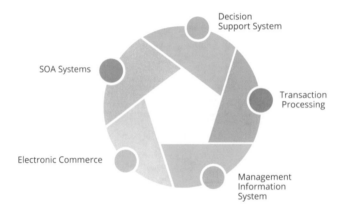

Decision Support System

SOA Systems

Transaction Processing

Electronic Commerce

Management Information System

simplilearn

Hardware Failure

Hardware Failure

It is a malfunction within the electronic circuits or electromechanical components

Hardware Failure

Encryption

Physical Security

Media Sanitization

Maintenance

Hardware Failure

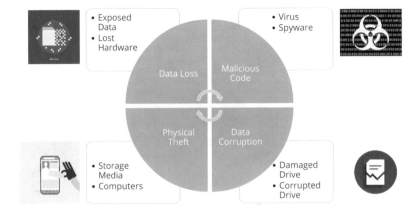

- Exposed Data
- Lost Hardware

Data Loss

Malicious Code

- Virus
- Spyware

- Storage Media
- Computers

Physical Theft

Data Corruption

- Damaged Drive
- Corrupted Drive

Hardware Failure

Error reports	Availability reports	Utilization reports (automated)	Asset management reports
Detect failures and provide corrective actions	Check downtime caused by inadequate facilities and excessive maintenance	Document the utilization of machine and peripherals	List the network inventory tools and their connected equipment

Host-Based Security

Host-Based Security

Host security refers to securing the operating system from unauthorized access.

Host-Based Security Controls

Host-Based Firewalls

Intrusion Detection System

Antivirus

Disk Encryption

Regular Backups

Access Control

simpl**i**learn

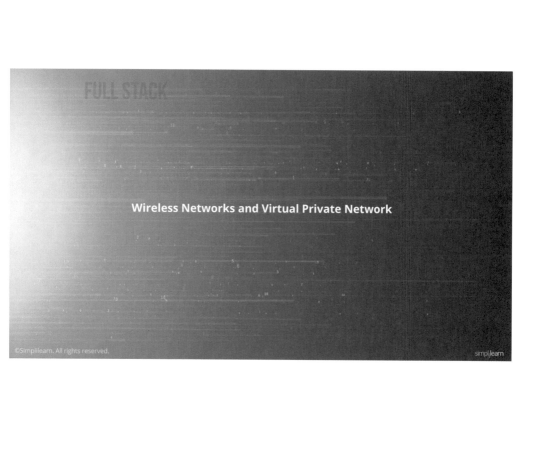

FULL STACK

Wireless Networks and Virtual Private Network

simpli**learn**

Wireless Networks

Wireless networks are computer networks that are not connected by cables of any kind.

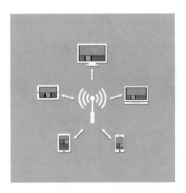

Wireless Networks

 Benefit:

 Drawback:

Benefit:	Drawback:
Mobility	Speed
Network Reach	Security
Flexibility/Scalability	

Wireless Attacks

Pose challenges to
security professionals

Easy setup at the cost of security

simpl‹learn

Wireless Countermeasures

Use encryption

Use Antivirus

Use WPA3
authentication

Turn off SSID

Change the
password

Case Study: Wireless Attack

Tel Aviv free Wi-Fi network was hacked. One notable example of how easy it can be for a hacker to take over a Wi-Fi network comes from Tel Aviv.

Case Study: Wireless Attack

The free Wi-Fi network of Tel Aviv was hacked.

It incorporates basic security controls to keep users secure in the network.

Case Study: Wireless Attack

Tested its security controls

Noticed a new Wi-Fi access point

Discovered an HTTPS port 443

simpl**i**learn

Virtual Private Network

VPN extends the corporate network securely via encrypted packets sent out via virtual connections over the public internet to distant offices, home workers, salespeople, and business partners.

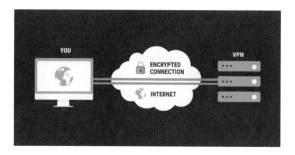

Virtual Private Network

Increases the
network span

Accesses their
corporate enterprise

Communicates with
business partners

Helps in being efficient
and effective

Helps grow their
business

simpl*learn

Types of Virtual Private Network

Intranet VPN

Extranet VPN

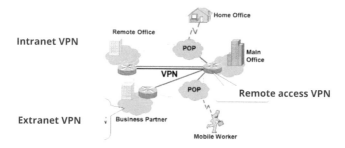

Remote access VPN

Virtual Private Network

Lack of required host
security software

Physical access

Endpoints

Man-in-the-middle attacks

Hardware limitations

simpl**i**learn

VPN Risks

Strong user
authentication

Host identity
verification

Security posture
validation

Secure desktop

Configuration
considerations

Education and
awareness

simplilearn

Wireless Network Example: Bluetooth

Speed is 2.4 GHZ and range
is between 10 to 30m

Introduced in 1994

Uses radio waves for
communication

Short-range wireless
communications technology

Bluetooth Attack Example

Bluejacking is the unauthorized sending of text messages to a nearby Bluetooth device.

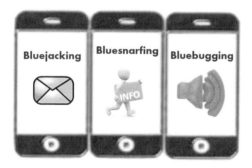

Bluetooth Countermeasures

 Use Bluetooth for confidential information

 Change the default PINs on your devices

 Do not leave your devices in discovery mode

 Turn off Bluetooth when it's not in active use

simplilearn

Bluetooth Vulnerability: BlueBorne

It is a set of nine exploitable Bluetooth vulnerabilities.

It affects every laptop and mobile device.

The airborne attack is difficult to protect.

Radio-Frequency Identification (RFID)

simpl;learn

Radio-Frequency Identification (RFID)

RFID uses radio waves to read and capture information stored on a tag attached to an object.

RFID Risks

RFID Security Controls

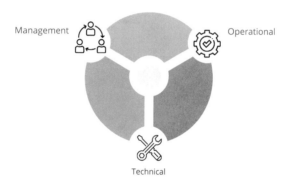

Management   Operational

Technical

Case Study: RFID Hack

Mobile Keys and Bluetooth

Uses near-field
communication (NFC)

Guests download an app
to their phones

Opens the door with
signals

simpli**learn**

Emanation Security

It is a hardware or electronic device that emits electromagnetic radiation.

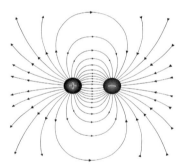

Controls Against Electronics

Faraday Cage

White Noise

Control Zones

Network Security Controls

Network-Based Security

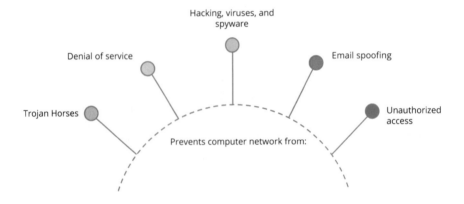

Hacking, viruses, and spyware

Denial of service

Email spoofing

Trojan Horses

Unauthorized access

Prevents computer network from:

simpl*learn

Network Attack Categories

Active attack

An intruder initiates commands to disrupt the network's normal operation.

Passive attack

An intruder intercepts data traveling through the network.

Firewall

Stops hackers from
accessing network

Controls network
traffic

Allows users to access the
internet

simpllearn

Firewall Features

Is a combination of hardware and software

Controls the vulnerable point between a corporate network and the internet

simpllearn

Unified Threat Management (UTM)

UTM combines several key elements of network security to offer a comprehensive security package to buyers.

Unified Threat Management (UTM)

 Goals

- Simplicity

- Streamlined installation and maintenance

- Centralized control

 Issues

- Single point of failure

- Single point of compromise

- Performance issues

simpl[i]

Web Application Firewall

Filters, monitors, and blocks HTTP traffic

Filters the content of specific web applications

Prevents attacks from web application security flaws

simpl**i**learn

Intrusion Detection System (IDS)

Intrusion Detection System otherwise known as IDS is monitored network usage anomaly.

- Works together with firewalls and routers

- Operates in the background

- Alerts when intrusions are detected

- Protects external and internal misuse

simpl|learn

Intrusion Detection System Components

Sensor

User Interface

Analyzer

Admin Console

Intrusion Detection System Categories

**Network-based IDS
(NIDS)**

An intruder initiates
commands to disrupt the
network's normal operation.

**Host-based IDS
(HIDS)**

An intruder intercepts
data traveling through
the network.

Intrusion Prevention System (IPS)

- Closely related to IDS

- Designed to detect and prevent attacks

- Must be properly configured and tuned to be effective

Network Admission Control

It is a concept of controlling access to an environment through strict adherence and implementation of security policy.

Network Admission Control Goals

Prevent/reduce
zero-day attacks

Enforce security policy
throughout the network

Use identities to perform
access control

simpl**i**learn

Honeypots

A honeypot system is a computer that sits in the screened subnet or the DMZ and attempts to lure attackers.

Enable services and ports

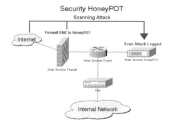

Have services emulated

Honeypots

Group of honeypots implemented together is called a honeynet.

simpl**i**learn

Security Testing

Vulnerability Scanning

It is a process of examining your systems and network devices for security holes and weaknesses.

Vulnerability Scanning

Vulnerability scanners are designed to help administrators and address vulnerabilities.

Vulnerability Scan Goals

- Identify vulnerability

- Identify lack of security controls

- Identify common misconfigurations

Some scanners are capable of remediation checking for misconfigurations.

simplilearn

Penetration Testing

Tries to exploit the system

The most aggressive form of
security testing

Uncovers any weaknesses within
the environment

Simulates an attack from a
malicious outsider.

Emulates the same methods
attackers would use

Types of Penetration Testing

The types depend on the organization, its security objectives, and the management goals.

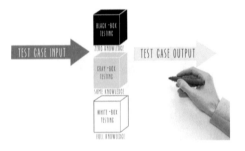

Types of Penetration Testing

In black box testing, the tester has no knowledge of the internal design or features of the system. It simulates the external attacker the best.

Types of Penetration Testing

In white box testing, the tester has complete knowledge of the internal system, it may yield a more complete result, but it may not be representative of an external hacker. It may be a good indicator of an internal type of threat.

WHITE-BOX TESTING

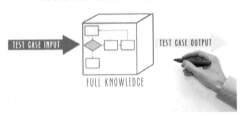

Types of Penetration Testing

In grey box testing, some information about internal working is given to the tester.

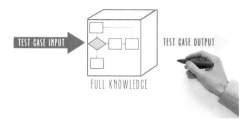

WHITE-BOX TESTING

TEST CASE INPUT

TEST CASE OUTPUT

FULL KNOWLEDGE

- Helps guide tester tactics

- Mitigates the risks

simplilearn

FULL STACK

Security Audits

simplilearn

Security Audits

These are systematic evaluations performed with the purpose of demonstrating the effectiveness of controls to a third party.

Security Audits

It is performed by independent auditors. Auditors provide unbiased view of the state of security controls.

Types of Security Audits

- It is performed by an organization's internal staff.
- The reports are intended for internal audience.

Disadvantage: Conflict of interest and hidden agenda

- It is performed by third-party auditors.
- The reports are intended for third-party stakeholders.
- NDA is a prerequisite.

Disadvantage: Cost

Key Takeaways

- Networks are part of a large, centrally managed, internetworked architecture solutions.

- Wireless networks are computer networks that are not connected by cables of any kind.

- Network-based protection or security is a method of preventing your computer network from unauthorized user access.

- Security testing is a process of examining your systems and network devices for security holes and weaknesses.

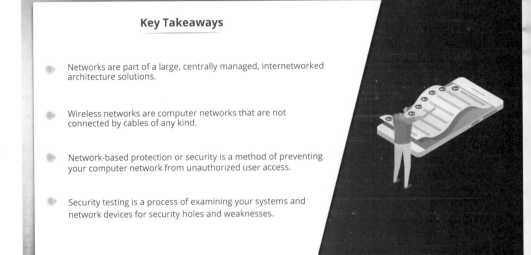

simpli**learn**

Made in the USA
Columbia, SC
09 June 2024

36380101R00046